Kayla Martell Feldm
Jewish poet currentl
a Genesis Poetry Slam winner, and has had work commissioned by JW3, Canada Water Theatre, Watch Your Mouth at Holbeck Underground Ballroom in Leeds and Vashti Media. She has featured regularly at Spoken Word London, Extra Second London, Pussy Liquor, and Homos and Houmous, and was invited to take part in the Roundhouse Poetry Weekender led by Bridget Minamore and Cecilia Knapp. In 2021, she co-founded the Sovereign Writers Group, a collective of six writers who work across stage, screen, poetry, and prose to share skills and develop new work.

Outside of poetry, Kayla is a writer and director for stage and screen. She was a Co-Founder and Co-Artistic Director for Snapper Theatre, an Associate Producer for Maiden Speech Festival, and is a regular teacher and director at Identity School of Acting. She has also worked as a literary associate for Abingdon Theatre Company in New York, a theatre scout for Theatre503, and a script reader for Hampstead Theatre.

Writing with a focus on themes of identity, family history, mental illness, and womanhood, Kayla has taught spoken word poetry workshops at the Leeds chapter of JLGB and at Limmud Conference, where she was invited to present poems from this collection in 2019. She premiered her first spoken word solo show, HEAR ME OUT, at Maiden Speech Festival, where it sold out and garnered five star reviews, later transferring to Camden People's Theatre as part of Calm Down, Dear Festival.

Printed by Book Empire
www.bookempire.co.uk
Unit 7, Lotherton Way, Garforth, Leeds LS25 2JY
Printed in Great Britain

First printing, 2021.

www.kaylafeldman.com

Cover illustration and design by Jessica Sinclair
www.jessicapoetart.com

TIKVA

KAYLA MARTELL FELDMAN

For Gary

&

For Yarden, Raya, and Menachem

Content Warnings: gun violence, child abuse, self-harm, suicide, mental illness, and the untimely death of children

CONTENTS

ONE STEEL CABLE: A PROLOGUE

In September 2012, I went off to study at the University of Leeds. Most of my friends had already started university, were about to start, or were younger and still finishing their A-Levels. The one friend left behind was Keren, who, having relied on her considerable natural intelligence to coast through school, had barely studied for her exams and ultimately didn't get the grades she needed for university. Never one to wallow or be discouraged by failure, she simply found another way. She wanted to study French, so she moved to France for two years and worked. She retook her exams, got straight As, and accepted a place at the University of Warwick to study French. She and I wrote letters to one another throughout my first two years at university. In July 2014, as I was preparing to move to Montreal to study on exchange, and Keren was about to finally begin her studies at Warwick, she sent me off with a pack of twelve letters: one for every month I would be away. This was the first letter.

~

Dear Arnold[1],

However we phrase it, twelve months is a long time. But in a way, I'm glad we've been living in different places for the past two years. It means that I know for certain that however long we're apart, when we're together again nothing will have changed, at least, between us. It's because we've spent this time apart that your going isn't killing me nearly as much as when you were getting ready to go to Leeds for the first time. I can't describe to you the pain of accepting the fact that you were gone from me. Because

[1] This is an inside joke. We were 12, and, well, you probably had to be there.

even though we were still in contact, and you weren't very far, and however much we thought otherwise, you were moving on with your life and mine was in stasis.

Geographic distance has nothing on the distance that was between us then. For me, at least, we were occupying different dimensions. However much we spoke or were near to each other, we could not occupy the same space.

The letters you sent me were lifesavers. In that time which was the closest to nothingness I had ever been, your letters showed me light in the future but didn't blind me with it. They showed me the joy you had, I could have too, all the while acknowledging I couldn't partake in it right then. They gave me hope, when I could so easily have lost sight of any feeling. In that time, your letters were the only things that made me blame myself a little less, made me hate myself a little less. So yes, you saved my life.

And after being pulled back from that abyss, anything was possible. So, we didn't hang out on a daily basis. So what. So, we were separated by land and sea, thousands of miles. So what. So, we were living different lives. So what. You don't need a thousand threads when you have one steel cable.

Even when it's coming up to ten years that we've known each other, I'm still not sure what that steel cable is. But it's not really important. What's important is that I have you and you have me and if you need anything, anywhere, anytime, if you're in Canada or in the Antarctic or from 50 years in the future, I'm right here, whether 'here' is France or Mars or up in the sky.

Now, this time, when you're packing to go to Canada, you're not leaving. Not me, at least. You're a little bit further than usual, but I'm not worried. You're going to have an absolutely amazing time and you're going to put pictures on Facebook and when I look at them I'll be right there with you, looking in awe at the scenery, drinking Canadian beer, telling you to get a move on with the hot Canadian you're making out with, and laughing at your poor French grammar.

I can't wait for you to tell me all about it, although I'm going to pretend to be all disinterested to cover up the fact that I'm crazy jealous. But you'll see right through it, as you always do.

I love you so much, and although I know you're coming back, I'll still miss you like the Keren in Year 7: Like crazy.

All my love.

I

When in doubt, the answer is always Mark Twain.

Feldman family motto

~

The world blows up and everybody dies.

Feldman family catchphrase

NOTHING RHYMES WITH MOTYLINSKY

When my great-grandfather came to America,
crossed an ocean with some
misguided notion of freedom,
the clothes on his back,
and a sack full of dreams,
it seems he was misled.
At the border, they asked for his name.
He said:
Isador Motylinsky
A phrase that had throughout his life
rolled from his tongue with every shaken hand
in this land was
foreign.
They said:
Welcome to America, Irving Martell.

Just as well,
a name now famous for its strength,
for the princes on the silver screen,
Less *foreign*, more *exotic*
Their accents not so different from my ancestors'.
He left Hungary,
hungry for a life his parents never had.
Sad to leave home
but welcomed into this new one
by the stone lady and her promise:
Bring me your hungry, your tired, your poor!
By God, he was.

Over a century passes.
Isador Motylinsky is forgotten
by generations of Martells.
We swell with pride at the sound of our name!
The same as Oberyn, champagne, and
that Very Superior Old Pale cognac, but
no matter, no matter!
That name is *ours*.

Only it's not.
It's a black spot on our history,
a tick on a box marked *foreign*,
the wick on the candle of Lady Liberty's flame;
a name given arbitrarily by other foreigners
who just happened to get there first.

Where *Motylinsky* is mumbled
like marbles in the mouth
Martell comes from deeper South
A belly feeling,
reeling with
excitement, not uncertainty.
A tapestry of bright futures,
Adventures, battles won,
A song sung with a fist in the air.
Not the blank stare of an immigration officer.

It's not so uncommon
to be forgotten in this way,
To be changed or exchanged
for something with a little more *oomf.*
Donald Trump was *Donald Drumpf,*
Marylin Monroe was *Norma Jean,*
Ciccone completely left behind
when *Madonna* hit the scene,
It's not so beyond comprehension
that the tension between history
and mystery
gets pulled so tight.

Isador Motylinsky had no choice.
His voice was lost in a sea
of a thousand foreigners,
His name left behind
like some sign of failure.
Over a hundred years later,
his new name becomes part of mine.

I wear *Martell* like a badge of honour.
Isador was father to Sidney,
Sidney married Minnie,
and their first daughter is a Martell too:
Mother to me.
Their second is now a Daneman
but I suppose it's all the same to them
because when a woman marries,
it's expected that she carries the name of another.

Martell
A name at the end of my mother's
and in the middle of mine
in time will die out too.
Is it really dying to leave behind a name
that was never truly mine in the first place?
Am I lying by omission
every time I say my name in full?
Perhaps we have simply evolved,
moved with the pull of the tide,
reclaimed our given identity,
Left the old one behind.

CANTICLE

My childhood is
Harry Potter books one to three
read by Stephen Fry
and book four
read by Jim Dale.

My childhood is
the Sunday Puzzle on NPR
with puzzlemaster Will Shortz and
A Prairie Home Companion
narrated by Garrison Keillor:
The News From Lake Wobegon
was the only news I cared about.

My childhood is
cassette tapes of Dad reading Dr. Seuss books
so even on business trips,
we were never left wanting at story time.
To this day
I cannot fall asleep to silence.
I am accustomed to drifting off
to bedtime sounds:
To the *Shiloh Trilogy* on tape,
Little House on the Prairie,
101 Dalmatians and *Aladdin*
on crackly VHS.
As an adult, I nod off to Netflix,
Audible,
Radio 4 podcasts.

My childhood is
the songs we sang
as we pedaled bikes laden with camping gear
through the forests of rural Maryland,
The rhythm of the wheel of a mountain bike
speeding through dirt,
The chatter of its spokes,

The heavy click of the gears shifting,
The jarring crunch when the chain popped off.
I don't remember the smell of oil on my fingers
as I jimmied it back on,
I remember only what it sounded like once fixed.

Parsley, sage, rose-mary and thyme.
Well before I knew the scent of any of these herbs
my childhood was infused with their melody
in my father's voice.
His song
Our Song.

My childhood is
the maternal melody of my godmother
singing Hebrew in a Texan accent,
Stirring English phrases into the Shabbat prayers:
Hamotzi lechem min ha'aretz
We give thanks to God for bread
Our voices rise in song together
As our joyful prayer is said.
I can still recite
the birkat ha'mazon in full.
The *Match of the Day* theme
will always be Adon Olam to me.
My childhood is less the smell of besamim, more
Yai dai da da da da dai dai
Yai dai da da da da dai dai
Yai dai da da da da dai dai
Da da dai dai,
Da da dai.
Havdalah is still
the closest I ever get to spirituality.

My youth is full of noise
and I have sewn in patches of silence
where I would rather forget.
It speaks volumes.
Memory is clever that way.

In amongst these melodies of my childhood
is a Simon & Garfunkel tune, stuck in my head
since my Dad first sang it to me.
Silence … grows.

TEN FEET TALL, CAN FIGHT BEARS

When I was a kid,
I'd take the big white t-shirts out the laundry;
The ones that smelled like my dad.
He worked long hours, so
by the time he got home
he just smelled of the tube.
The shirts came down to my knees.
On hot days,
I'd run through the garden in bare feet.
The shirts would end up back in the laundry
covered in mud and grass stains.
By then, they just smelled of me.

When I was a kid,
my dad made up bedtime stories on the spot.
Maybe that's where I get it from.
He'd invent our adventures,
make up giant bearded garden gnomes
and flying pianos.
I never heard the endings
His soft voice and Michigan lilt
is like a lullaby.

It's hard to write about my dad.
He was the hero of my childhood.
His job title was God of the Universe,
tagline: *Ten feet tall, can fight bears.*
He was and is the king of Dad jokes:
I'll never forget
him nearly ripping out his hernia stitches
with his own light chortle.

As a kid, it is easy to assume
that your heroes are unbreakable.
As a kid, it is easy to blame them.
As a grown-up, it is difficult to stop.
Forgive me, Father.

AFTERSHOCK

The first time she finds home
she is six years old,
four thousand miles from where she was born.
She is at ease for the first time in her life.
Her home is a cardboard cut-out,
A storybook illustration,
The picture that comes with the frame.
It has five bedrooms
too large for the small children,
with bunk beds for one.
A basement fit for adventures,
where cardboard boxes become
pirate ships, mazes, obstacle courses.
A front yard with a big tree for climbing,
to hang a sky-chair from.
Her home is the cabins at summer camp,
running wild in the woods,
the banks of a shallow creek,
makeshift showers in campsite water pumps.
Here is where happiness comes easy.
After two years, she will be forced to leave.

In therapy,
I learn every happy childhood memory I have
exists between September 2000 and August 2002.
Two years
is all I have to show for my happy inner child
before her universe begins to crumble.

When she is ripped from her home,
she is returned to the place she was born.
Everything is off-kilter now
and she is out of sync.
She has outgrown
the five-bedroom house
with the basement and the big tree
that is now home to someone else.

This house has been home once before
but there are cracks in the walls now.
She follows one with her finger
all the way from one end of the house to the other
but she cannot find where it begins or ends.
She finds a crack in the ceiling one day,
and as she follows it,
it splits open.
Her parents' marriage splits open.
Crack.
She finds a crack in the bathtub.
Her sister leaves the country.
Crack.
She pulls back the corner of her bedroom carpet
and discovers cracks there
from an earthquake she remembers as a child.
She switches bedrooms.
Four thousand miles away,
one car collides with another
and both car and family are split open.
Crack.
Crack.
Crack.

In therapy,
I learn about the last time I was happy.
That there is no returning to a home that has been destroyed.
The earthquake
that shook my childhood bedroom
has followed me through the decades.

IT COMES

it comes wet and fast
hot and sweetsour like gunmetal
and I think of my uncle's Glock 19 9mm
that he pulled on me once as a joke
I never liked guns like my uncles like guns
say it makes them *walk taller feel stronger*
to me it seems like power comes from
having something thick to swing
when your arms lose momentum
our running joke that *Feldmans can't throw.*

feel taller, walk stronger
as if the world wasn't already built for them
I think of where I come from
the same men with eight firearms between them
also travelled halfway across the world
to see my first aliyah
to be there personally to cheer shekoyach
as I dismounted the bimah at thirteen.

my aunts are pacifists
an inner-city Englsh teacher, PhD
and a children's heart transplant nurse
heroes to the *n*th degree
sometimes I wonder how many times
they've swallowed how they really feel.

to put sex and my uncles in the same poem
feels disingenuous (I've never fucked my uncles)
but to put cocks and guns in the same poem
does not
and every time I've swallowed
it's felt as much like love as gunfire
as much like love as violence.

TO MY MOTHER,

who never changed her name
despite the constant confusion
that hers was not the same
as her husband or her children.
Every time they pulled us aside
at airport security, I'd hide
under her skirt as she told them
I'm her mother.
No other woman would say that sentence
more often.
They'd soften
when they saw how I clutched at her hand
saw our blue eyes that same rare shade
and wave us through the gate.

To my mother, who understood *unconditional love*
to be the love for her children.
Her babies that she made, birthed and nursed
despite the fact that her husband came first
They called her curst,
I called her a mother.
My mother, who could never be trapped
under the thumb of my father,
would rather always be alone
than be known
as a wife before a mother.
A woman by any other name
would not smell as sweet.

To my mother, whose door was always open
even when I slammed mine shut
etched prayers into my skin
and when she begged to be let in,
I'd scream *fuck you* to the rafters.
After,
she would still hold me.

To my mother,
who in never saying *no*
gave me the tools to finagle
Made me able to debate
Convince me, she'd say.
Reason came and went with a gust of wind.
She was all I needed.
Her life, impeded by motherhood
side-tracked by infants who would
take all she had
and leave her, one by one.

This kind of love does not make her weak.
She's unique in breaking the cycle
of a beaten child who left her own unbruised.
Where love came to her
from the buckle end of a belt
Mine was felt
in hugs and kisses and smiles
miles away from her own family.
She ran away the second she could,
from the city that never slept
to the city that stayed weird,
fearing she'd never go home
but she made London home
eventually.

To my mother,
who after three children
made her home in a house
built on the ashes of a broken marriage
The rest is legend
as she tended to her nest like a magpie,
collecting love like coins and gold.
It's cold when the door's open
but I wouldn't have it any other way.

To my mother,
who picked up pieces

of other broken families
Sewed them into her skirt
like buttons.
It was sudden, when I left
but she is not bereft of family;
Her heart is the start
of a new one.
My friends will still sit at her table
and feel able to call her
Mum.

WOLFIE

When I was seventeen, I think I had no interest in doing anything with our family. You're lucky, you don't have a family to not do things with.

My sister says this to me when I am seventeen.
She is twenty-four
and has been gone for five years.
She, so much her mother's daughter,
ran away the second she could
from the Big Smoke
to the Holy City
and I will blame her for a decade
for leaving me behind.

My sister can be
tactless.
Takes after my dad's side of the family that way.
In this moment,
as she calls me a lone wolf,
without a family
without a pack
without a crew
I realise
how much she has missed.
How little she knows me now.

I am a proud member of
The Radiator Crew.
That's the group of us at school
that sit by the radiator in the music department
(the one that hums in B-flat)
every single break- and lunch-time
because we are *just cool that way.*
Except, obviously,
we are not cool.
We are, in fact, drastically *un*-cool:
This is the only thing we have in common.

This, and the fact that each of us comes
from a Broken Home.

My parents are divorced,
family split open across three continents.
These two sisters have different dads,
were raised by a single mum
whose cancer comes back when I'm in year nine.
One of them stays at my house each Thursday
as her mum recovers from chemotherapy.
This one's dad is dead.
This one's mum is dead.
This one's dad is estranged.
And this one…
well, his sister used to come here
but, she's dead now, too.

We all know what it's like
to have a family
more like a Build-A-Bear workshop
or a Choose Your Own Adventure book.
The nuclear ones from our maths textbooks
show mum-dad-daughter-son-dog/cat
and I never had a brother
so Eli becomes mine.
Now it doesn't make sense
to call him anything else.
Eleven years later
I still struggle to explain how
no, we don't have different dads, well, we do, but we also have different mums, and we only met when I was 8, and no, I'm not adopted, but he's my brother, and that's all there is to it.

Even now,
The Radiator Crew long forgotten,
my family takes in strays.
When our friend dies,
her sister becomes ours

and we adopt her parents as aunt and uncle.
When our friend's mum dies,
my mom takes him to see Fleetwood Mac,
calls him *son from another mother.*

So when my sister tells me
that I have no-one
it is the saddest thing she has ever said to me.
Not because I have no-one
but because I have built my own family
to fill the hole she left.
It has been easier to build a new one,
tangled and knotted and warped in places,
but whole,
than to repair the old one.

There is a magic in this.
There is a magic in knowing that family
is so much more than blood.
But there is magic, too,
in the blood that binds us,
and it would be years before I figure out
how to stitch my sister and I back together.

BABY

she loves bright flowers
always has a surplus of olive oil
now that she's gone
I'm forgetting to water the plants
eating more raw food
the dog eats when I do
his bowl stays full most days
it's hard not to feel abandoned
I waited too long to leave her nest
she said I'd always be her baby

ODE TO A NIBLING

To my future nibling, who grows in the belly
Of my big sister (who is very smelly),
You are, at the moment, just a cluster of cells
Growing at speed in our mademoiselle.
I am so excited for you to appear,
I simply can't wait until you are here!
Due in one hundred and fifty-five days
As the new year comes in
You'll be showing your face.
I am overexcited, I must admit
Because of all the great things to come,
You are IT!
So for you, in advance of your birth, I must gift
This small storybook for your spirits to lift.
Within its pages, I'm sure you will see
That the world in store for you, it will be...

FANTASTICAL! MAGICAL!
Full of GREAT FUN!
Full of games and of songs
That your parents have sung,
And of course, understand,
There will be sad times too
But in time, my dear, I trust that you
Will persevere through them
And come out on FIRE!
Not literally, of course, but on fire with desire,
On fire with passion, on fire with drive,
My dear, through the bad things, you will
SURVIVE.

Because that's who we are
And it's who you will be.
That's your mum and your dad,
Your Aunt Bex and me.
That's Grandma and Grandpa,
And that's Mimi too

And most of all, darling, that will be YOU.
You're entering into a tribe of survivors,
Of singers and dancers and epic high-fivers.
I love you already, you cluster of cells, you!
And I simply can't wait to in-person tell you!

IMA

My mother is here.
It is Shabbat, and my mother is here.
The candles are lit,
the challah is covered,
the Manischewitz has been poured.
There is rosemary and garlic in the air
as she places her hands on my head
and the heads of anyone present
whose parents are not
so she can bless them on their parents' behalf.
She has enough hands to bless everyone.
(she has like, six hands)
Despite having lived in Haifa for three years,
her Hebrew still drifts towards the Bronx.
Despite having said this prayer
every single Friday of our childhoods
and many more besides,
she still stumbles:

Ye-shmerech adonai
Ke-Sarah, Rivka, Rachel, v'Leah
Ye'verech'echa Adonai ve-yish'merecha
Ya'eir Adonai panav eileicha viyi-chunecha
Yisa Adonai panav eileicha
Ve-yaseim lachem[2] *shalom.*

I can do this without her.
I can roast the chicken and potatoes
the way she taught me.
I can even do the soup.
I can light the candles, cover my eyes
and sing all four verses of Shalom Aleichem.
I can pour the wine and bless it from memory

---

[2] When only girls/women are being blessed, this would be *lachen*.

at superhuman speed.
I can rip into the bread with my bare hands
like all Jewish children are taught to do.

But my mother cannot bless me from a distance.
I cannot be like Sarah, Rivka, Rachel v'Leah
without her say-so.
My cousins Sara v'Rachel
and my sisters Rivka v'Leah
do not need this weekly reminder
that they are special,
that they are warriors,
that they are the daughters of Yisroel.
They were named for the mothers of the tribes.
But without her hands on my head,
without her words of prayer and guidance,
how can I still be her daughter?

WHAT THE VACCINE ALLOWS

I hug my dad today
for the first time in 340 days,
give or take.
I am tentative, tearful,
gazing up at his new bionic eyes
as he pays for our coffees in the park.
I want a hug, I say,
without feeling, as he high fives my wellies
with his bigger hiking boot.

as a child, I'd leap into the arms
he'd have no choice but to throw open
carry me
as a teen, I'd elbow his shoulder
nudge it over mine
hold me
as a woman I lean my head against his chest.

are you scared of me? says dad
bionic eyes sliding out of focus
(I'm already standing too close)
his immunity does not shield him
from needing to hold his children
me ageing does not prevent him
from needing to fix me when I am broken
his arms are too weak now to be leapt into
but you cannot outgrow fatherhood

so I cross the last three feet
and let him pull me in.

HOME: AN INTERLUDE

I was born in water, in the dining room of 82 Alicia Gardens. My sister cut my umbilical cord and brought it into school for show-and-tell. At pickup, the teacher approached my father and said: "Your daughter's been telling fibs! She's claiming this is her sister's umbilical cord!" A pause. "What do *you* think is in the jar?" my father asked.

My first home came years later. A little neighborhood called Fox Hills, in Maryland, just a few miles from the Potomac River. Where I learned to ride a bike, before immediately crashing it into a parked car. By the creek where red leaves crunched underfoot in the fall, and cherry blossoms bloomed in the spring, with the clearest water you've ever seen. Where tiny fish would slip between rocks to escape our tiny, grasping hands, and at night, we'd hear cicadas shriek and sing, and in the morning, we'd find their discarded shells on the trees and in the grass, and we'd know it was nearly summer.

Back in London, my home became the bottoms of closets nestled amongst long forgotten dry-cleaning bags, and the cupboards above my bed where we kept extra sheets and pillows. Cool, dry, dark places. Good for storing rice or pasta or wedding china. Or small children seeking shelter from shouting parents.

When we moved house, and the cupboards were full, with no space for children to hide, I made homes where I could. The roof of the new house, where I'd sneak cigarettes as my mother slept. The empty, dark rooms at house parties where people were too drunk or too stoned to look for me. In the middle of the crowd in a dark venue with the bass pounding through my chest and to my toes; that sweet smell of sweat and raw energy where nothing else existed. Nothing but me, and the band, and the kiss of whatever person I'd found to worship me for an evening.

I made my home in the secondhand bookshops on Charing Cross Road, in the record store on Brick Lane, in noise-cancelling headphones with the volume turned up full.

I felt it in the arms of the first boy I loved; in his crooked smile and his crooked teeth and his crooked elbows and the weight of his body on mine. I see it in my mother's eyes that are twins with mine, and in that soft, lilting Michigan accent of my father's – his bedtime story voice. I hear it in the squealing giggles of the children I helped to raise, and how is it possible that they grew up so fast?

My home is on bookshelves, and in the audience of theatres, in airports and train stations and reclining armchairs. Under the summer night sky in the Colorado Rockies, the sky so clear and clean that every single star is visible, like someone with a can of spray paint took liberties with the Milky Way. In every key of my mother's piano, and in the battered body of my twelve-year-old guitar. In everyone I have kissed, every hand I have held, and everywhere I have walked.

Your home is my home.
Make yourself at home.
I feel so at home with you.

As if we carry them with us; memories, like snail shells, carried on our back in every step taken.

The weight never getting too much to bear. As they grow, we grow, making space for more, every inch a part of us, sewn into our skin. *Home is where the heart is.* And are we not at home? Gathered here, in some function room or bar attic, or tethered between the pages of a book. Where we share our homes, exchanging them, like hermit crabs scuttling from one to another, shedding our winter skin for something else. Still small children hiding in closets and empty rooms, making space for ourselves amongst the wedding china. Afraid, or maybe just uncertain, of what awaits beyond the door.

II

Madness Lies.

King Lear, Act III Scene IV

ART ROOM, 2011

I used to go and cry in the art room
it's soothing in there
smells of wood and paint and turpentine
no-one asks questions
they just smile with their headphones in
and paint

LET ME EXPLAIN

It's hard to explain, but
let me try.
I am high
on a drug that once felt orgasmic
caught in a phantasmic encounter
with the universe.
At first,
my fingers buzzed,
my lungs felt numb:
I was too dumb to notice
this meant I couldn't breathe.
My heart would seize,
pump terror instead of blood,
like wading through mud,
my legs not quite strong enough
to unstick my shoes.
I would lose
Every time.

It's hard to explain, but
let me try.
I am caught between two nightmares, and
the hairs on the back of my neck
warn of danger.
My stomach is lead, and
the dread of an unknown ghoul
is all that consumes my mind.
I might as well be blind,
or deaf.
That is the only way to run.

It's hard to explain, but
let me try.
My stomach is full of bees, and
my knees are made of wax.
P.S. I swallowed an olive pit last week so don't be
concerned if they start growing out of my navel.

This unhappy marriage
of depression and anxiety
is a lump in my throat
because I've swallowed my tongue.
It has hung itself
from the rafters of my uvula
and clung to my gag reflex like a leech.
Each time I vomit blood,
it gets a little looser.
It's hard to explain
because it's hard to understand
that the land I'm standing on always shifts,
and there's a rift between my normal and yours.
The tectonic plates between us quake
in the wake of my shaky state of mind.
We are close enough to touch,
and you are close enough to save me,
but I am a land mine,
so you don't.
You couldn't,
even if you tried:
The cause of my insanity is living.
I am giving what I can,
but it isn't much.
I am stuck in the eye of a hurricane,
and if I move an inch I'll be swept away
so I'll stay
where I am.
Every phone call is a klaxon, and
when the churchbells ring on a Sunday
it's a countdown.

It's hard to explain, but
I can't remember where I put my keys,
or when I ate last, and
I've been holding my breath for a year.
My body is here,
but it's a shoddy piece of work.

I'm not making sense.
I told you,
it's hard to explain.
These metaphors are all I have
and I'm sick of saying *fine*
when you ask me how I am.
I am miles away from fine,
countries away from normal,
a continent from
Good thanks, how are you?
It's hard to explain
when I feel like I'm dying.
I'd be lying
if I told you it was normal.

It's hard to explain, but
I'll try.

SOMETIMES

I think people avoid asking how I am
because they know I will no longer say
Fine.
I was not raised by British parents.
They were not stiff-lipped.
My loud New York mother
and my Detroit dad
taught me truth, above all else
(I was a bad liar as a child)
so I have learned to spell *colour*
and not to call it a *fanny pack*
but I would still rather say
Actually I'm awful because I'm depressed and the weather's a bit shit and I'm not sleeping well and I keep having panic attacks

OBSESSIONS

I'm scared I will

Kill my nephew
With my fingers
With my hands
Snap his neck
Drop him from the balcony
Drop him on his head
Break his arm
Break his wrist
Break his fingers
One by one
Throw him into a wood chipper
Put him in the microwave on HIGH
Get out of my seat in the front row, leap onto the stage, yell OOGABOOGABOOGA and do a dance
Get out of my seat in the front row, leap onto the stage and gouge out the actors' eyes with my bare hands
Get out of my seat in the front row, leap onto the stage, leap onto the actor and rape her
Him
Them.
Drop the pint I'm pouring
Reach across the bar
Slap the customer
Assault the customer
Call the customer a CUNT

I'm scared I am

Cutting
Peeling
Slicing
Being sliced, cut, peeled
Shitting in the street
Peeing in the street
In the middle of the sidewalk
In the middle of the road

In my neighbour's driveway
Naked

I'm scared I already am

Shitting in the street
Peeing in the street
In the middle of the sidewalk
In the middle of the road
In my neighbour's driveway
Naked

I'm scared I

Have left my body entirely
And I am doing these things without knowing I am doing them

I'm scared I'm

Saying words I'm not allowed to say
Would never say
N*****
R*****
P***

I'm scared of

Fucking my students
Wanking off my teachers
Fingering my boss
Sucking off my dog

I'm scared I

Want to
Want to
Want to
Already have

I'm scared
Am I
Do I
Have I
Will I

CRISIS TEAM

If you had been living with this for ten years without seeking help, you would have gone crazy by now.

COMPULSIONS

Loud music
Louder music
Full volume
Sing along in my head
Sing along out loud
La la la la la la la la
Cover ears
La la la la la la la la
Keep hands busy – cigarettes
Roll, smoke, roll, smoke, roll

Am I wet
Sit on the toilet
Am I wet
Check
Double check
Triple check
Is this what arousal feels like
Am I aroused
Am I
Aroused
Sweaty
Menstruating
Incontinent

Sit on hands
Clench fist
Crack
Investigate
Interrogate
Ask
Again.
Investigate, interrogate, investigate, interrogate
Research

Flinch

Hand covers bruise

There is no bruise

Hand covers breast

Finger over nipple
Make sure
But if it was happening, you would feel it
Toss, turn
Scroll through Netflix
Everything on Netflix
Organise
3am: go downstairs and eat as much as you can until you can't anymore and then have a cigarette
(Every night)
I can't reach the spot on my back being cut open
It isn't being cut open, you would feel it
Skin peeling back
Touch
Touch it, just make sure
I can't reach
Make sure
I can't reach
Can't breathe
Can't
Don't leave the house
It isn't safe out there
Sleep
If you can

LET ME EXPLAIN 2.0

It's hard to explain, but
let me try.
I lie awake at night
eyes as bright and open
as the screen beside me playing
Something.
Anything really
to drown out the hell in my head.
I can't tell if that's dread
or adrenaline
making my heart pound, but
the sound of mindless TV
will make it stop.
It will.
This time,
even though it literally never has before.

It's hard to explain, but
let me try.
Danger is everywhere.
I swear I'm not crazy
or lazy, but
this maze I've made is hard to navigate
and my compass is broken.
and my map is just crayon scribbles!
and I didn't bring enough snacks.
I swear I had a raincoat
but it's not
actually
waterproof.

It's hard to explain but
let me try.
There's a voice in my head
that doesn't belong to anyone.
Someone's put it there.
Made it sound like me.

After three affairs and a messy divorce
depression and anxiety
have somehow brought forth
a force to be reckoned with.
She was born breach.
Born backwards.
Born angry.
She has sunk her teeth into my breast,
nails dug into the sides of my head,
fed on my worst nightmares,
and lurked there
unseen
for ten years.

It is easier for me to think of her as *other*.
Another me,
a separate entity
I can't control.
I'm told that drugs can, but
I took diazepam for three days straight, and
she still kept me up all night.

It's hard to explain because
we're *woke* now.
I choke on every metaphor
because they're all shit
and let's face it:
We think we know everything by now.
I say *depression* or *anxiety*
try to be
out, open, answer questions,
raise awareness
but if I told you what she puts in my head
you'd lock us both up for good.
Even though
I hear it every day.
I'm a bit OCD
because you're tidy, or
picky, or

you just really like right angles
as she tangles her fingers through my hair
pulls tight, and
I lose sight of everything I am.
Drift.
Sift through everything she says, and
search for evidence of what I'm not.

I'm not a paedophile.
I'm not a rapist.
I'm not a murderer.
I'm not suicidal.
I'm not gonna fuck my dog,
or push that old lady into oncoming traffic.

But if I've met you,
I've thought about killing you.
What you look like fucking your girlfriend.
Or me.
I can't stand still on a train platform
Hug the walls
Just in case.
I can't hold my nephew for too long
Just in case.
The longer you talk,
the less I'll look you in the eye.
Spend an hour in my head
and you'll be sliced open six ways to Sunday.
She puts blood on my hands, and
I can't stand to check if it's all mine
but *I have to.*

It's hard to explain obsessions
when you can't see my compulsions.
It's hard to explain that these thoughts
aren't mine, and
I'm running out of ways to say
It's all in my head.

HOPE

is literally my middle name
and I will still sift through dozens of haystacks
looking for it.

DURING THE DUMPSTER FIRE,

remember the puppies.
Or whatever small animal
most tugs at your heartstrings.
Remember them doing things like
yawning,
dreaming,
yowling their first too-high too-quiet yowl.

Remember that there are pancakes
for every dietary requirement,
and that strawberries are always in season
somewhere.
Remember that you can have your eggs
any way you like:
With a kiss, if you're lucky.
Remember that soldiers out of uniform
can always be dipped.

During the dumpster fire,
remember not to burn your poems.
Or, if you must,
memorise them first.
Recite them from the rooftop
as the flames climb to the top floor
and immortalise yourself in metaphor:
The ashes of your words will be carried
by the wind, over to the next city,
or country, or continent, or hemisphere, or
planet or galaxy or

Universally fucked.
We are universally fucked.
Remember the music that screams
almost as loud as your soul is screaming
right now.
WE ARE SO, SO FUCKED!
It screams.

Scream back.
Sing off-key.
Whisper sweet nothings and
fall behind dancing.

Remember that there is a choice
between cake and death,
and that the restaurant at the end of the universe
has a pineapple upside-down cake to die for,
and I just might!
(I'm allergic to pineapple.)
Remember that *Tories*
is just one letter away from *Stories*,
and you are a better writer than Boris.
Remember that you can spin anything into gold
and everything he touches turns to

Ashes
is all that's left after the flames.
So during the dumpster fire?
Do everything else.

PURE

The morning after it happens,
I'm sitting outside
and I notice
the birds.
There are birds in my garden.
I am noticing the birds in my garden, and
I remember your story about the hummingbird,
when you didn't have your camera
and here was this bird,
a once-in-a-lifetime moment
you couldn't capture,
so you wrote it down and kept it
and no-one can take that away from you.

The morning after I break,
I'm sitting outside
and I notice
the birds
and I don't have my camera either.
It's only a moment
but it's a pure moment.
If there is anything pure in this world
it is this moment.

There will be moments like this again.

If there is hope to find,
I will find it in these moments.
If there is hope to get better
I will be reminded in moments like this one.
There will always be birds in my garden.
When I can't get out of bed,
when I can't leave the house,
when I am scared of my own imagination

There will be moments like this again.

LETTERS TO GARY: AN INTERLUDE

10th February 2014

Dear Gary,

They told me to write a letter to someone I was no longer in contact with, a letter saying something I never got the chance to say in person. At first, I thought of Alex and Sam, because I always, always do. And then I remembered how, the last time I saw you, an unexpected appearance at my sister's wedding, you told me that you think of me often. That I remind you of them. That, watching me grow up, you've been able to glimpse what they might have been like today. And then I remembered the last time I saw you before that – you told me you were sad that day because you had finally mustered the courage to start clearing out the boys' bedroom, and you weren't quite sure what to do with all their toys. I was scared you might ask me to help you, but you didn't. And then I remembered the time before that, when you didn't even recognize me because I had just hit puberty, and had grown about a foot and a half and wore make-up. That time, you told me I should be grateful that I had such a wonderful father, and that you missed being a dad. The time before that, you called me on the phone the day after their funeral. You didn't call your sister or your friends or your aunt. You called me, because you said I had a special relationship with the boys. Because I was the closest thing they had to a sister. The closest thing you had to a replacement. I've realized that, of all the people I've lost contact with, losing you was by far under the worst circumstances. You didn't die, but you branded me as the talisman of your own personal tragedy. We look at one another and no longer see family and love and change, but rather, we see the greatest tragedy in both our lives. The very sight of you brings me to tears, and I cannot forgive you for cutting me out of all the happy parts of your life. You never call me on my birthday, but only on the anniversary of their death. You never ask me about school, or my job, or my relationships, you merely reminisce about what theirs might have been like. You no longer see me as myself, but as a ghost of what you lost. We have not spoken about anything real in almost a decade. I miss you.

Love Always.

~

29th April 2019

Dear Gary,

Two years ago, you remarried. I found out from the photos on Facebook and I will admit I was a little shocked. I spoke to your sister and she said she *also* found out from photos on Facebook, so I won't take it personally. You always said you wanted to die having had only one wife, that Judy was irreplaceable, but it's understandable that your life is moving on. That *husband* is a better word than *widower*.

It's been a while since we last spoke. A few years. I thought I might see you when I was in Michigan in September – we went to your sister's for Rosh Hashanah – but I didn't think to call. I haven't thought to call in a long time. It's been five years since I wrote that last letter and, re-reading it, I feel a little guilty. To be so unforgiving and yet to do nothing to reconnect. Connecting with you is difficult, I'll admit that. In that last letter I expressed such bitter resentment at being made the "talisman of your own personal tragedy" but, if I'm honest with myself, I've done the same. And it's been so long now that I'm uncertain where to start with reconnecting.

Where do I begin? My adulthood has been riddled with death in the same way my childhood was. My adulthood so far has been difficult – challenging, and changing. I'm not sure I'm the adult they would have become. I listened to the tape again recently, for the first time in a while, and it is odd to hear myself so young. As young as they were, as they will always be. My accent is different – will become different. Their voices hadn't broken – will never break. It is like hearing ghosts. Like hearing an adult put on a child's voice.

I don't believe in ghosts. So I hope you will accept my apology for treating you like one. For treating you like the ghost of my past, of the past tragedy we share, and for being angry with you for grieving, and remembering in your own way. I would say I forgive you, but I don't think there is anything to forgive. I think we have been ghosts to each other for a long time.

There is so much to tell you. I don't know where I should begin. But one of these days I'll send one of the dozens of letters I've written you, or better yet, I'll pick up the phone and call. I hope you're well. I hope you're happy.

Love Always.

III

Energy cannot be created or destroyed. It can only be changed from one form to another.[3]

First Law of Thermodynamics

---

[3] My father, an engineer, has argued with me at length about the accuracy of this statement, and whether it was a quote from Albert Einstein, or the very thing his work disproved. Regardless of who is correct, I find it an apt and comforting sentiment – physics be damned.

POEMS FOR THE DEAD

You left behind your stamp collection
in albums and boxes,
thousands, perhaps
but I never counted.
It was the only connection we had.
Stamps, and
the name you gave me.

~

Blood on his hands.
Cold,
encased in steel.
He will rot
for what he did
and his son
will grow up without a father,
just like their father
grew old without his sons.

~

You are remembered
in Dairy Milk and Nutella
and *Doctor Who* reruns
and a drawing of a scribble
and a tree in your garden
with branches thick enough
to bear the weight of a small girl.

~

They said you were fine.
You were not.

~

Skin like crumbling wax,
white hair, rarely washed,
and a look;
the blank gaze of someone
who does not know who or where
or what they are.
You were terrifying to me.

~

Your grandmother cried loudly at your funeral
and I held her hand to keep her standing.
There is a question mark beside your death,
although I did not know that at the time.

~

I remember you by your hair.
I was a child,
and there were too many relatives.
I kept track by identifiers;
you were Harvey, with the hair.
A long, brown braid
with grey streaks as I grew older
(and by default, so did you).
Chemo claimed your hair
before cancer took your life.

~

A breeze is stronger higher up.
Even stronger when you're falling.

EPITAPHS

(1)

Sylvia Feldman:
First-generation American citizen
with Russian in her blood
and Yiddish on her tongue.
She was
A crossword connoisseur,
A maker of mouthwatering Mandel bread,
A thespian 'thusiast,
An HRC voter,
A voracious reader.
Sweet enough already, she said,
to take her coffee without sugar.

(2)

She was born a Cohen:
Her priestess status stripped from her.
In Judaism, there are only priests.
Her father, her brothers.
As she and her sister fought for education
one at a time,
through 1930s Detroit depression winters,
her brothers walked on hallowed ground.
Will meet again in ha'Olam ha'Ba
As righteous men,
As holy ghosts,
As high priests
in the Temple of Jerusalem.

THINGS WE FOUND IN MY GRANDPARENTS' APARTMENT

Twenty-five years of *National Geographic* issues. Ten years of *Better Homes and Gardens*. A further decade's worth of financial magazines. Several clocks, toasters, and other non-working appliances Poppa never got around to fixing. Calendars and diaries from dozens of charities they supported. Pens. Pencils. Dust bunnies. Tumbleweeds. Playing cards. Several thousand used stamps. Assorted stationary with hotel letterhead. Matchbooks from New England restaurants. Matchbooks from Yonkers restaurants. Matchless socks. Pamphlets. Yarmulkes from every bar and bat mitzvah they had attended since the late 1920s. Two daughters. Five grandchildren. A taxi company.

You can't take it with you.

TWELVE YEARS

Somewhere in the last twelve years
I became a grown-up, and
sewn up in the memories of this awkward shift
from child to wild and somehow back again
is every single memory of you.

Somewhere in the last twelve years
I stopped believing in god,
fell in and out of friendships,
grew hips and an ass,
fit a size eight shoe,
hit five foot two – and kept growing
not knowing that with every inch
I was sowing seeds
of a future you would never get.
I set myself a list of challenges, ticked boxes like:

Land a lead role
Fall in love
Get high
Skydive
Graduate (twice)

I sift through junkyards in my mind
and shift perspectives in corrected colour.
I have tried
to keep the sight of you clear,
as near and dear to me as my own life
but every frame is riddled with cigarette burns;
the picture turns the wrong way
and crinkles at my touch.
No matter how I try to hold it,
the photo fades.
I had no idea that living fully
meant erasing parts of you.
I remember you pure.
Children always are.

In the last twelve years
I have been to hell and back
lacking any roadmap or compass.
I found home eventually.
I have lived a life I couldn't share with you.
With every new adventure
I censure my joy because it isn't ours.
Your death sours everything I achieve.
I spend my days in rehearsal rooms
and try to place you in the ensemble
but your voice will always be that of a child,
mild and light
with a slight hint of melody
sung only to me.
The voice of a boy, and not a man,
because you never got to be.

You have now been dead
as long as you were alive.

Half a life sentence.
A sixth of *his* total time.
He will die behind bars
but of old age,
not the rage he mixed with drink,
and my soul sinks at that sobering thought
but I cannot wish him dead
because he has a son your age.
A son who will grow up.
Show up to the parts of life you couldn't.
Become a man.
He will set his own list
and check his own boxes,
sow his own seeds,
and know with every step
the one clear thought I have every day:
That we are living,
where twelve years ago
you stopped.

TAPE

I keep you in my poems
because I'm not sure where else to put you.
You were too young for a cell phone, so
there was no number to call
to listen to a repetition of you
over and over
until the line clicked off.
If there had been,
I can't imagine the bill I'd have racked up.
But there's a cassette tape
in a box in the back of my closet
with possibly the last recording of your voice.
You are older on that tape than anywhere else.

I REMEMBER YOU

young.
All sharp elbows and floppy hair,
not a care in the world except
soccer, and
peanut butter sandwiches, and
Saturday morning cartoons.

I remember you with grass stains
and growing pains.
In a way
you're a museum exhibit in my head:
Not dead, but fixed in time.
You stay mine that way.
You stay nine that way.
You stay how I remember you.

WHEN ALL THIS IS OVER

For you, I mourn a friendship
snatched in its beginning.

We first met
at the birth of your niece.
My friendship with you existed only in pixels:
Facebook messages,
likes and comments,
fondness,
at a distance.

We met for the second and third time
at the shiva for your mother.
You knew it was coming,
but that never makes it easier.
Losing a mother is
Unwriteable.

When all this is over, come for dinner.
When all this is over, we'll go to a gig.
When all this is over, I'll take you to a poetry slam.

Grief burned through your body,
or so we thought.
Grief does not burn as quickly as fire.
As quickly as cancer.
Grief is a slow burn.
Grief is a match.
Cancer is a forest fire.

From beneath you, it devours.

We met the fourth time
in the oncology ward at Queen's Hospital.
I brought a bag full of nail polish
and we painted each of your nails
a different colour,

sparkles on top.
We hugged you as gently as we could.

When all this is over, come for dinner.
When all this is over, we'll dance at the wedding.

When we met the fifth time
I knew it would be the last time.

A month later,
your nails still sparkled.
We could not hug this time,
not even gently.
I squeezed your hand
and into that squeeze, I put
all the times I would not get,
all the times you would not get,
all the times we would not get.
Gigs
and spoken word nights
and vegan dinners
and festivals.
And then I let go.

When all this is over

"I'll see you at the wedding."

LEVAYA

The morning we bury her
I take a photograph of my brother
on the mirpeset.
The hills are on one side, the ocean on the other
but in the picture, you can only see the hills.
He does it because I've asked him to
and I tell him he doesn't have to smile.
I don't know how long I have left
to take pictures of the people I love.

There is no precedent for this.
If he's annoyed, he doesn't show it.

We stand side by side
in front of the bathroom mirror.
He unties and reties his tie.
I clip and unclip my hair,
and then decide to just leave it down.
A week later I'll cut it off because
who cares, it's just hair.

We go, and
Mom says we're going to see a body.
I think maybe this will make it real, but
I've never seen a body before.
Not a body that's just
just a body
with nobody in it.
She's wrong though, it's a box.
When they roll it out,
It's too narrow.
She couldn't possibly fit in there.
Her body is bigger than that.
She wasn't that thin, she

Her sister says
I saw her. She's in there.

She says she'd never seen a corpse before.
That word.
She looked good, she said.
They washed her hair.
She said she touched her face,
and my first thought is
I wonder if she was cold?
She must've been?

The service is only half in English
and if I had any energy at all
I'd concentrate on translating in my head but
I tune out until I hear my name and
chavera.
Someone puts their hand on my back
and it takes me a moment to move.
I check my pockets and panic
you'll find it, the man says, and I do.

I realize that most of these people
won't have known her like I did.
I won't have known her like they did.
Baby
Niece
Little one.
I tell them what I do know.
I look over at this too-small box
I promise her I will carry her with me forever.
I tell her I love her.

The only time God is mentioned
is when we say Kaddish at her graveside.
and then I watch
as her grandfather
rolls up his shirtsleeves.
The six blurry numbers on his left forearm.
I watch as this man, who survived:
Auschwitz
The death of a four-year-old son

The loss of a sister
And a wife
in that order
picks up a shovel
and fills his granddaughter's grave.

ASTRONAUT VS. DEEP SEA DIVER

You asked
not who would win in a fight but
which I'd rather be
if I had to.

I said I'd take the bullet.

Last night I dreamt of the ocean
being thrown into a clear aquamarine net
with a ray swimming underneath.
Woke up terrified.
Remembered what day it was.
One day a year to face fears and foes and
familiar faces forcing frowns:
Fifteen years today.

I'd rather both than this.

A LITTLE LIFE

I tell stories for a living.
She saves lives for a living.
I can say that storytelling is lifesaving
but she spent four hours
resuscitating a hamster with a hairdryer once,
felt her physically come back to life,
and, *man*.
That's a rush I can't begin to imagine.
A little life
coming back.

When our dog was dying
she could smell it.
She knew before I did.
I clung to him as long as I could,
desperate to keep him with me
keep him running,
walking,
until the day I carried him to her surgery
and she held him as he went.

But when our friend died
neither of us could explain it.
All her knowledge and expertise,
every minute of her studies and practice
suddenly useless
and we held each other and howled
through that incalculable loss.

When our friend died,
our dog was in his last days.
He wandered the house
searching for the source of the trauma.
He limped from room to room on arthritic legs
never settling,
searching every corner for the unseen villain,
his low whine the only constant

as we went from howls to silence.
On Christmas Eve,
he gave up his search,
and shat all over the living room carpet.

We made our home a haven
for everyone longing for our friend.
Made a space for telling stories.
Stories of her.

Our dog had a little life.
A little life of running
and walking
and treats
and more snuggles than he could handle.
His little life was full of love, but not much else.
Our friend, though.
She swallowed the world.
That's what her dad says.

We buried her beside her grandmother
three thousand miles away.
I heard stories at her funeral
that I'd never heard before
and I told them some of mine.
About the time in Sicily when she swam out to some rocks with me because she knew I was a weak swimmer, but she didn't want me to feel left out.
About the time she ran out in a thunderstorm, twenty minutes out of her way, to bring us chocolate because we were sad.
About the book she left me, the inscription:
I am forever with you.

Our dog died the day after Boxing Day.
His kidneys had stopped working.
When your kidneys stop working
there is nothing filtering the toxins

from your body
so they build up
and make your breath smell like ammonia.
The stench is unbearable.
Our house smelled of death
long after he stopped breathing.
I survived his death because
she saves lives for a living.
She knew how to warn me,
how to explain.
He died in the arms of someone who loved him.

Our friend died eleven days earlier.
A bus hit a car
and a tiny, insignificant little aneurysm
flooded her brain with blood
before she knew what hit her.
No warning.
No-one to explain.

But we survive her.
We survive with stories.
Stories of her, and how
in the little life she was given
she swallowed the world.

THERE ARE TREES

The day we buried you
despite the forecast for rain
we insisted it be sunny
and so it was.
We wore purple
brought boots in case of mud
but there was none.

Above your headstone
there is a tree
whose branches reach just far enough
to shelter you, and only you:
Your own personal tree.
The tips of its lower leaves stretch
to the edges of either side
where your parents will rest someday.
It opens itself to them
as you would have done.
As you will do
when they are ready.

At the service,
instead of returning you to god
as a spirit or an angel or
something else you didn't believe in
we returned you to the earth.
The man explains
the first law of thermodynamics
the transfer of energy
from your body into the soil,
how over time
your energy will spill into the roots of the tree,
and your sister and I laughed
because she has a PhD in physics
and it wasn't *all we needed to hear,*
but it was something.
She will be a tree someday,

she said.

There are trees
where you are buried,
and in the sun on that day
the colours were brighter,
and I imagined you there
perched amongst the branches.

Once we had finished
filling the earth over you,
we laid flowers there.
I laid mine in the middle,
where your belly would be
where I would rest my head
as we read together.
The softest part of you.

She will be a tree someday.

There are trees
where you are buried
and I failed physics
so I don't know how long it will take
but one day
some day
You will be among them.

ORA

[After Sarah Kay]

If I should have a daughter, I will name her
Ora:
Light
and she will be.

My mother says she feels you with her
as she watches the sunset from the mirpeset.
Hills on one side,
ocean on the other.
When we went on holiday to Brighton,
I sat on the beach
and wrote a postcard to your sister
P.S. The sun is shining and I imagine she is here.
At your funeral,
I said your parents named you appropriately,
that you were the
ray of light
in every room.
We added *light*
because *ray* was not enough.

So if I should have a daughter,
I will make her in your image.
She will have blue eyes
and curly hair,
Untamable
and I will tell her how I tamed it for you
on your 22nd birthday,
in four hours with a very powerful hairdryer.
I will find her a Spanish tutor,
the one language you didn't get the time to grasp.
I will teach her to cook
with the recipes you showed me.
Her vegan birthday cake
will taste every bit as soapy as yours.
Her lullabies

will be the two hundred songs you left behind
and the ones we wrote together.
She will read.
Oh, will she read.
She will read the books we shared
and the ones you recommended
that I never bothered with
until after you were gone
and I couldn't tell you how much I enjoyed them.
She will read the one you left me,
once I have mustered the strength to.

If I should have a daughter,
I will take her on the
Keren Brody Restaurant Tour of Bordeaux,
follow the business cards you kept
of every one you visited when you lived there.
I will take her to Korea,
because you always wanted to go and never did.
We will eat Bibimbap
(The dish you cooked me that last day)
and listen to Fake Love by BTS
(The song you played that last day)
and we will collect business cards
and ice cream spoons
everywhere we go.

If I should have a daughter,
she will never learn to subdue her laugh.
She will laugh how you laughed:
loud,
shrieking,
squealing.
Her laugh will not be stifled.

If I should have a daughter,
I will tell her everything I know.
She will have extra sets of grandparents
and an extended family of dozens

and she will learn that *family* is not *blood,*
That family is
A steel cable
A thousand threads
Hundreds of miles
Photographs
and Stories.

If I should have a daughter,
she, too
will swallow the world.

MILESTONES: AN EPILOGUE

Dear thirteen-year-old me,

I greet you from The Future. The year is 2019 and in two months, we will turn twenty-five, your next milestone year.

Thirteen is the age you become a Jewish adult. At thirteen, you have lived in two countries, been to three schools, and learned to *push the spaghetti down in the pot or it will set on fire.* You have learned that *feminist* is a dirty word. You have learned that you will never be good at maths. You have become accustomed to bereavement because you have experienced more of it at thirteen than any child should have to.

Sweet Sixteen, with its questionable history of debutante balls and parading young women before eligible bachelors. At sixteen, you will have learned that you are good at maths when you have a teacher who cares enough to say: "This is what you are currently achieving. This is what you *can* achieve." You will start the year with a C, and end it with an A.

Eighteen is the year you will learn about privilege. *Feminist* will stop being a dirty word, and you will claim it proudly. You will realize that most eighteen-year-olds north of Birmingham have never met a Jew. You will make your home in libraries, building them in every bedroom you move to. This thirst for knowledge will become your greatest weapon.

Twenty-one. Two more countries will become home and you will learn the art of solitude. You will learn which of the friends you have now will be the friends you have for the rest of your life.

The year is 2019, and this year, we will turn twenty-five. Another milestone year: the quarter century.

At thirteen, you have promised to be Best Friends Forever with a girl whose laugh reaches a pitch previously known only to dogs. This laugh, this shriek of delight, this squeal of pure joy, will annoy you and entertain you in equal amounts. This laugh is infectious, and you will catch it. Her grandfather will be the first person you meet with a number on his arm and this will be the first time you understand where you come from. Her mother will tell you that you lack discipline, and this will give you the strength to rebel, to question, to analyze. Her sister will write music just for you. Her father will build you bookshelves. You will take so many photographs of her. She makes faces for other people, but for you, she smiles. She will write a song for you and play it in front of the whole school. She will write you letters and fill them with confetti. She will bake you so many cakes. For your twenty-fourth birthday, she will give you a book inscribed with a note that tells you she is *forever with you*.

There is so much to come, and she – this girl, this sweet, kind, beautiful girl – will be there for all of it. You will spend so much time apart. She will move away, and you will move away, but you will always return to each other, this bond between you unbreakable by distance. She will teach you the most important lesson you will ever learn: that you are needed. You have promised to be her Best Friend Forever, and this will be true. But her forever will be shorter than yours. You will wake up one morning without her.

On what would have been her twenty-fifth birthday, you will pick up someone else's children from school and take them to the library, where you will watch the older one read aloud to the younger one and feel so proud at how much she is improving. How, two months ago, reading was just homework, and now it is an adventure. How quickly she has grown. The milestones she is already hitting. You'll take them home, help with dinner, and then their mother will take over and you'll go straight to *their* house. *Her* house. Her parents will feed you dinner and force you to have seconds and the three of you will cry together because this should be a happy day, a day of cake and songs and wine, a milestone day. A milestone she will never get.

But *you* will. In two months you will turn twenty-five. Milestone. In five years, thirty. Another milestone. Fifty. Milestone. One hundred. Milestone, and a letter from the Queen.

Or maybe you won't. Maybe today is the last day, and we don't know it yet. Because, how could you know? How could you have known? Let's pretend for a moment, then, that this is the last day. Me, on a stage, speaking to a room of friends and strangers and her thirteen-year-old self. What will be left of us when there are no more milestones?

Thirteen. The year you get your first job, as a part-time nanny for two wonderful children – a boy and a girl who will become so much more to you than just a job. Eight years later you will make a speech at that girl's bat mitzvah and tell her everything you have learned by twenty-one.

Sixteen. The year you help a boy in the school play gain his confidence. He will be quiet and cripplingly shy, but you will notice him, encourage him, practise his lines with him. When the play is finished, his mum will call your mom to say thank you.

Eighteen. The year we will all go to university except for her. You will write her letters so she doesn't feel abandoned, and three years later she will tell you they saved her life.

Twenty-one. The year you help a refugee from South Africa tell her story. The year you start sponsoring Guide Dogs.

If today is the last day, these milestones will be enough[i]. You have taken from and given to the world. You have learned and taught small lessons. You have grown and made mistakes and burned bridges and been both hateful and wonderful, but mostly, you have been good. You have made a mark.

The year is 2019. You are twenty-four years, ten months, and three days old. You will get at least this much. Here's to making every moment count. To being a positive force for good in the world. When the road you are travelling on is not leading you where you want to go, be bold and take the road less travelled. Remember your old friend, and that one steel cable. Here's to the future, to whatever is left. L'Chaim.

---

[i] Dayenu!

NOTES ON THE TEXT

Home was originally commissioned by Watch Your Mouth at Holbeck Underground Ballroom in Leeds, February 2016.

Pure is inspired by the work of Rose Cartwright.

In *When All This Is Over,* the line "losing a mother is/unwriteable" is inspired by Sara Hirsch's *Oranges and Lemons,* and the line "From beneath you, it devours" is inspired by *Buffy the Vampire Slayer.*

Milestones was originally commissioned by JW3 for their 2019 International Women's Day event 'Back to Bat', a re-imagining of the bat mitzvah speech.

Many of these poems were presented in a reading at Limmud Conference in 2019, prior to publication, and several originally appeared on my Instagram account @kaylatmf.

All the Hebrew and Yiddish words used in this book are Googleable.

ACKNOWLEDGMENTS

With endless amounts of gratitude to Finn Dobson who first introduced me to spoken word poetry, to my editor (and big brother) Eli Keren, to Jessica Sinclair for her beautiful and considered cover illustrations and design, and to the following people who read drafts and provided invaluable feedback and support in the creation and editing: Evangeline Dickson, Lucy Foster, Tyrone Lewis, Sara Hirsch, Eileen Martell, Howard Feldman, Elle Dillon-Reams, Rick Dove, and Dan Simpson.

With love to the PBOD, the Sovereigns, the Leeds Lads 4 Lyfe, and to Shira Kaliski and Adam Fox for being my home during the dumpster fire.

With appreciation and adoration for my sisters and their children, who give me hope every day.

With thanks to my agent Jennifer Thomas, who represents me for my theatre and film work *outside* of poetry, and for whom I thank my lucky stars every damn day.

In loving memory of Sidney A. Martell, Emily Weiss, Leah Israel, Minnie Martell, Rivka "Rikki" Wolfson, Harvey Auslander, Gil Albin, Sylvia Feldman, Alex Weinstein, Sam Weinstein, Judy Weinsten, David Novan, Keren Brody, and Arthur the Dog. May their memories be for a blessing and a revolution.